Supercross

Rev It Up!

Jackie Golusky

Lerner Publications ◆ Minneapolis

Lerner Publications Company
An imprint of Lerner Publishing Group, Inc.
241 First Avenue North
Minneapolis, MN 55401 USA

For reading levels and more information, look up this title at www.lernerbooks.com.

Main body text set in Billy Infant Regular. Typeface provided by SparkType.

Photo Editor: Annie Zheng

Library of Congress Cataloging-in-Publication Data

Names: Golusky, Jackie, 1996- author.
Title: Supercross : rev it up! / Jackie Golusky.
Description: Minneapolis : Lerner Publications, 2023. | Series: Lightning bolt books. Dirt bike zone | Includes bibliographical references and index. | Audience: Ages 6–9 | Audience: Grades 2–3 | Summary: "Supercross racers zoom around turns and soar over jumps on indoor dirt racetracks. Learn about their gear, their bikes, and what it takes to win these exciting races"— Provided by publisher
Identifiers: LCCN 2022011640 (print) | LCCN 2022011641 (ebook) | ISBN 9781728476322 (library binding) | ISBN 9781728478746 (paperback) | ISBN 9781728483269 (ebook)
Subjects: LCSH: Supercross—Juvenile literature.
Classification: LCC GV1060.1455 .G65 2023 (print) | LCC GV1060.1455 (ebook) | DDC 796.7/56—dc23/eng/20220421

LC record available at https://lccn.loc.gov/2022011640
LC ebook record available at https://lccn.loc.gov/2022011641

Manufactured in the United States of America
1-52213-50653-7/5/2022

Table of Contents

Ready, Set, Go!

Racers line up against the gate. The 30-second card rises. It tells riders that the race will start in about 30 seconds.

The 30-second card

Turning the card sideways means the race will begin in the next five to 10 seconds. Riders hold down their throttles. They're ready to go!

Supercross racers get off to a fast start.

The gate falls, and the riders speed forward. Most racers want to start in the middle. Then they have a straight path to the first turn.

The racers jump and turn around a dirt path. Supercross fans love to see dirt bikes in action.

A Supercross racer flies through the air after driving over a jump.

All about Supercross

Supercross is a type of Motocross. Motocross is an outdoor dirt bike race with jumps and turns.

Supercross races are inside stadiums. Trucks haul dirt into the stadium. Workers shape the dirt into turns, bumps, and jumps.

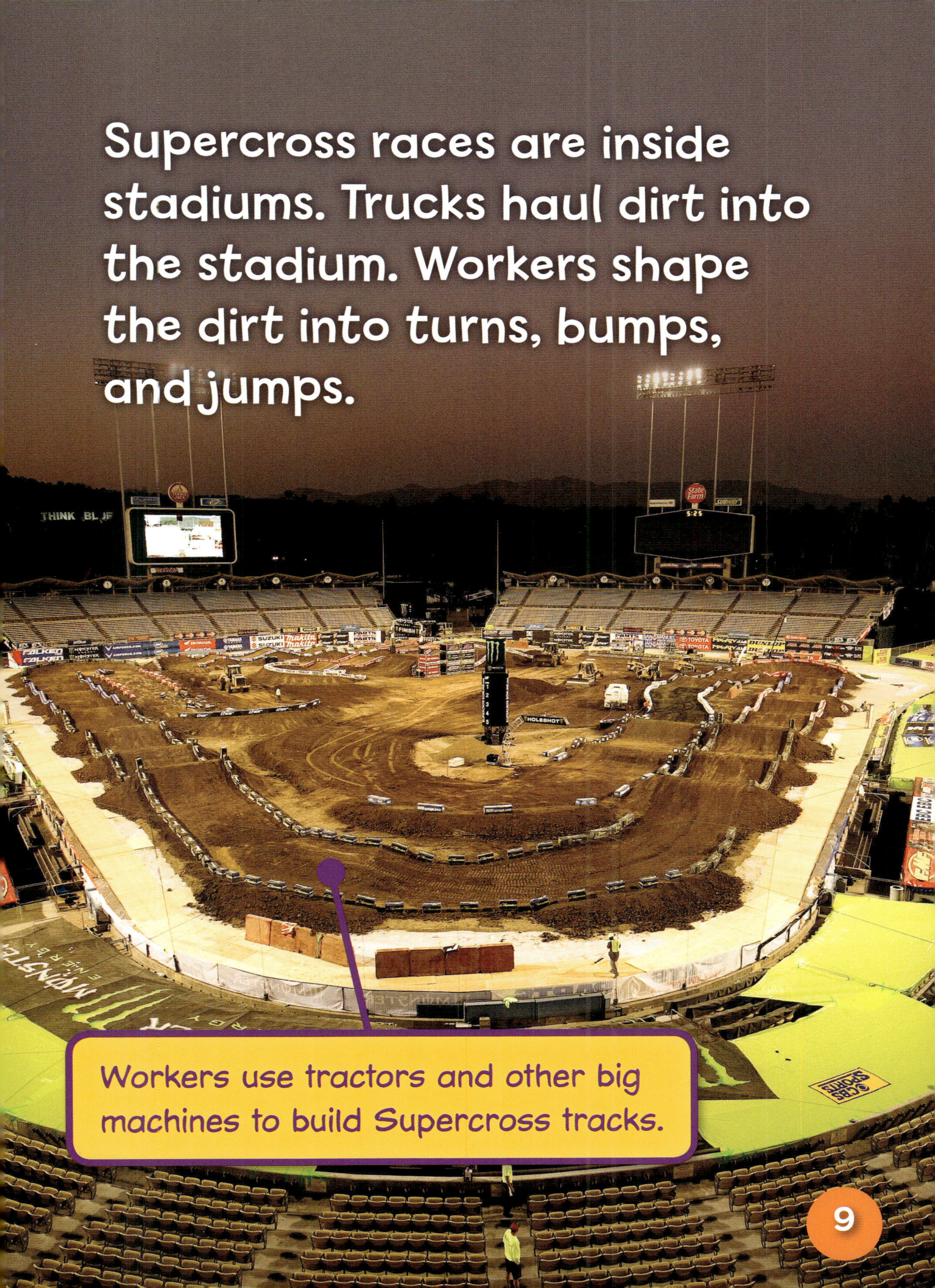

Workers use tractors and other big machines to build Supercross tracks.

Supercross races might be 15 or 20 laps. Some races are timed. Riders zoom around the track for 15 or 20 minutes.

In timed races, riders try to complete more laps than other racers do.

The 40 fastest racers continue in the event. They form two groups. The best racers of both groups make it to the final race.

Supercross racers zoom around a track in Salt Lake City, Utah.

Super Bikes and Gear

The most common Supercross bikes have 250cc or 450cc engines. Bikes with 250cc engines are light and easy to control.

A rider races with a 450cc engine.

Bikes with 450cc engines have more power. They can zoom out of the gate faster.

Special gear protects this racer from flying dirt.

Supercross is dangerous. Riders wear helmets to protect their heads.

If Supercross riders crash, their gear can protect them.

Supercross riders wear gloves, goggles, and body armor. Special boots protect their feet. The boots are light so riders can move easily during races.

Stars of the Sport

Riders from across the US meet at the Supercross Futures AMA National Championship. They race against one another for money and prizes. The best rider wins!

Eli Tomac has five Triple Crown victories. Triple Crown riders receive a score for each of three races. The rider with the top combined score wins.

Tomac's tires send dirt flying at a race in California.

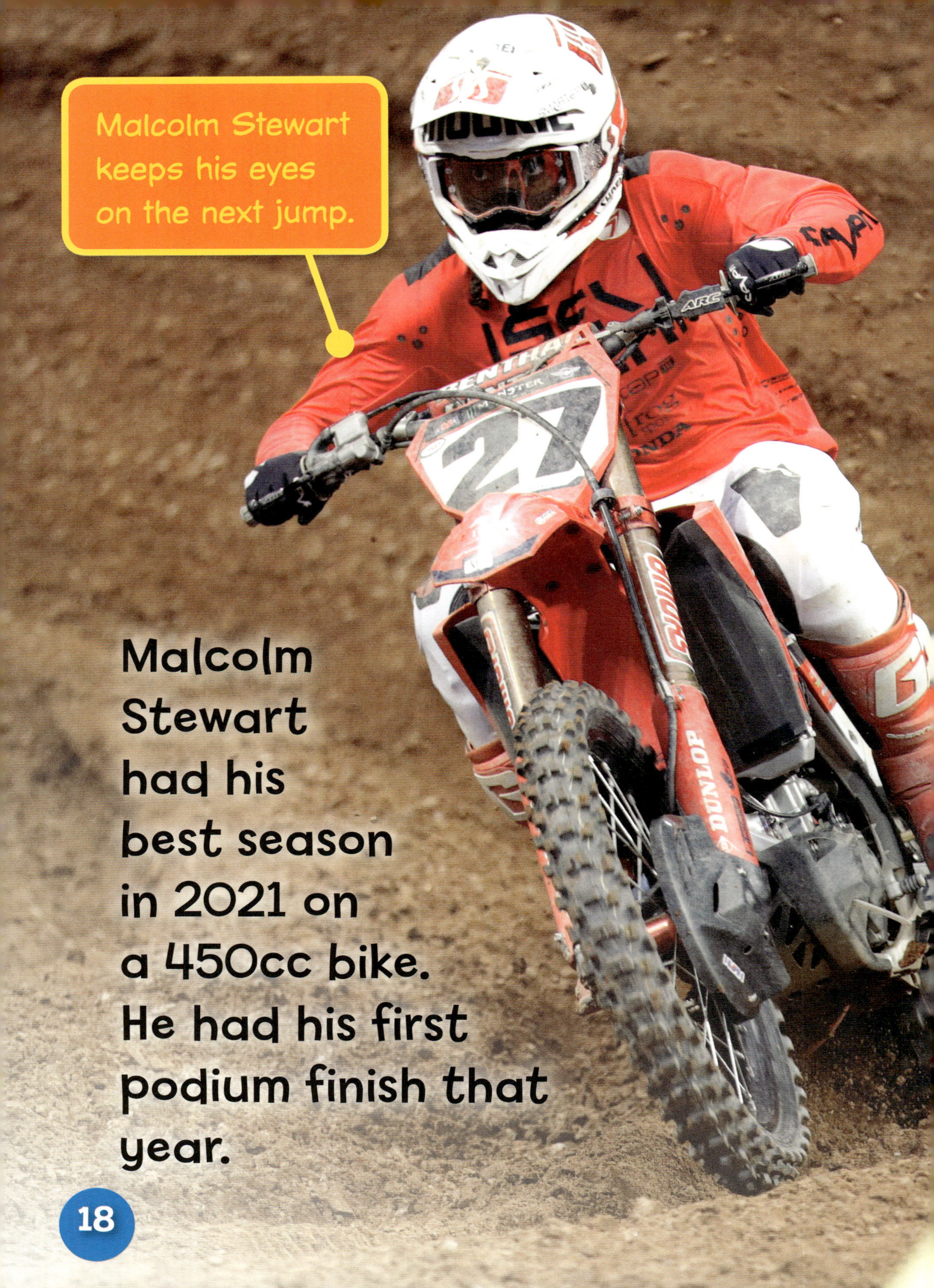

Malcolm Stewart keeps his eyes on the next jump.

Malcolm Stewart had his best season in 2021 on a 450cc bike. He had his first podium finish that year.

Jordan Jarvis has won more than 50 major Supercross races. She won nine AMA National Championships. Supercross fans can't wait to see what their favorite racers do next.

Fans fill the stands to see their Supercross heroes in action.

Bike Diagram

Kawasaki KX450

How It Works

How do workers create Supercross tracks? They place more than 5,000 sheets of wood or plastic on a stadium floor. Trucks dump about 26 million pounds (12 million kg) of dirt. The first layer of dirt is packed down tightly. Then workers shape the rest of the dirt into a track. They start with the outside of the track and work in.

Glossary

armor: a strong material worn to protect the body

engine: a machine that changes energy into motion

gate: a barrier used to start a Supercross race

lap: a trip around a racetrack

Motocross: a type of dirt bike racing where riders compete on an outdoor track

podium finish: placing within the top three of a race

throttle: a device that controls the flow of fuel to an engine

Learn More

Ducksters: MotoX Motocross
https://www.ducksters.com/sports/extrememotox.php

Golusky, Jackie. *Motocross: Rev It Up!* Minneapolis: Lerner Publications, 2023.

Hudak, Heather C. *Motocross.* New York: AV2, 2021.

Super Cross Live: Eli Tomac
https://www.supercrosslive.com/riders/450sx/eli-tomac

Van, R. L. *Yamaha Dirt Bikes.* Minnetonka, MN: Kaleidoscope, 2019.

Index

Photo Acknowledgments

Image credits: AP Photo/Lyle Setter, pp. 4, 6; AP Photo/Charles Mitchell, pp. 5, 15; AP Photo/Ted S. Warren, pp. 7, 14; AP Photo/Jeff Roberson, p. 8; AP Photo/Mark J. Terrill, p. 9; Jeff Kardas/Getty Images, pp. 10, 11; Tom Pennington/Getty Images, p. 12; Charles Mitchell/Icon Sportswire/Getty Images, pp. 13, 18; AP Photo/Andrew Bershaw/Icon Sportswire, p. 16; AP Photo/Thurman James, p. 17; Baptiste Fernandez/Icon Sport/Getty Images, p. 19; betto rodrigues/Shutterstock, p. 20.

Cover: Tim Clayton/Corbis/Getty Images.